Table of Contents

Yorkshire area of England was known for having fine animals, and it is thought that the Yorkshire Terrier was no accident but rather the result of purposeful mixing between a variety of terriers, probably including the Waterside Terrier, Clydesdale Terrier, Paisley Terrier, rough-coated English Black and Tan Terrier, and perhaps even the Skye Terrier and Dandie Dinmont Terrier.The Yorkshire Terrier doesn't look like a product of the working class, nor do they look like a dog who protected the home from rodents, but they were both. In fact, the

By 1880, Yorkshire Terriers had come to America, but the breed varied so much in size that there was great confusion around how big a Yorkshire Terrier might be. Many of these early Yorkies weighed between 12 and 14 pounds. By 1900, people on both sides of the Atlantic had decided that the small size was preferable along with a longer coat. Today, the modern Yorkshire Terrier is one of the smaller and most luxuriously coated dog breeds. These traits, along with their terrier heritage, have placed them as a consistent favorite with families. Breeding Yorkshire terriers is something a lot of Yorkie owners want to experience at least once. However, because of their very small size, the mating of Yorkshire terriers, followed by the pregnancy, and delivery of the puppies, are all somewhat challenging stages. Worry not though, most breedings and deliveries are seamlessly happening as long as you are informed. C-sections have to be expected and if you are wondering how to breed Yorkies, you need to understand that health comes first. Periodontal health for the dog, genetic testing, patellar luxation, and many conditions are frequent within the breed. As a soon-to-be Yorkshire terrier breeder, it is your duty to clear your dogs from these conditions. Yorkshire Terrier breeding is a fulfilling experience but read up on our article to be equipped with modern knowledge. That way, you will save yourself a lot of time and accidents.

The Waterside Terrier was one of their early relatives; these were small blue-gray dogs with fairly long hair, usually weighing around 10 pounds, brought from Scotland by weavers. Because of their modest roots, the Yorkshire Terrier was initially looked down upon by other wealthier households with dogs. Even the most snobbish could not deny the breed's obvious beauty, however, and in short order, Yorkshire Terriers were gracing the laps of wealthy mistresses.

CHAPTER ONE

WHAT IS A YORKIE?

A unique combination of terrier and toy dog. Starting out as a smallish terrier in Scotland, the Yorkie was brought to Yorkshire, England, by Scottish weavers and miniaturized into a true lapdog size. But lapdog doesn't necessarily mean all Yorkies like to sleep on laps all day. Some Yorkshire Terriers are indeed dedicated cuddle-bugs. But others act more like tiny terriers, with instincts to chase anything that moves and warn off strangers with a sharp shrill bark. As a trainer and behavioral consultant, the biggest problems I see with Yorkies have to do with how their owners treat them. If you carry your Yorkie everywhere, you're telling him that you think the world is too terrifying for him to walk around in.

Yorkies are bright little dogs who enjoy learning tricks. This lovely girl is clipped in a short coat that looks great and is super easy to maintain.

Don't treat your Yorkie like a doll to be carried or cuddled for hours. Do obedience training with him. Build him a tiny obstacle course. Teach him to play fetch with a cherished toy or ball. Above all, make sure he behaves.

When treated sensibly, most Yorkies are lively and inquisitive, physically and mentally quick, and spend much time trotting around the house and yard, checking things out.

Now, you do need to take precautions! There are indeed dangers lurking everywhere for toy dogs. The trick is to let your Yorkie walk on his own four feet as much as possible, while still keeping an eagle eye out for real danger.

If you don't protect his safety, he can be hurt or killed, but if you baby him and don't require him to stand on his own four feet and be well-behaved, he can end up insecure or downright nasty

This is NOT a breed to allow off-leash. Too much can happen to these small creatures in the blink of an eye. Larger dogs may view him as a delicacy and he is just brave/foolish enough to charge toward them, bellowing threats in his high-pitched voice. Plus he has excitable chasing instincts and will chase birds and butterflies across the road.

If all this sounds like Yorkshire Terriers are too active for your taste, rest assured that even the go-getters are lovers of comfort who enjoys snuggling into soft pillows periodically through the day.

YORKSHIRE TERRIER

Small in size but big in personality, the Yorkshire Terrier makes a feisty but loving companion. The most popular toy dog breed in the United States, the "Yorkie" has won many fans with their devotion to their owners, their elegant looks, and their suitability to apartment living. Even though these are purebred dogs, you may find them in the care of shelters or rescue groups. Remember to adopt! Don't shop if you want to bring a dog home.

Although Yorkies can make for great apartment pets, they also have a tendency to be yappy, which neighbors may not appreciate. They'll need a bit of maintenance too, especially when it comes to dental care. While these pups are playful, they're also small and can be injured by children. But if you can provide lots of love, attention, care, and playtime, you'll have a loving, adorable companion who'll stick to you like your shadow!

Breed Characteristics:

Adaptability

- Adapts Well To Apartment Living
- Good For Novice Owners
- Sensitivity Level
- Tolerates Being Alone
- Tolerates Cold Weather
- Tolerates Hot Weather

All Around Friendliness

- Affectionate With Family
- Kid-Friendly
- Dog Friendly
- Friendly Toward Strangers

Health And Grooming Needs

- Amount Of Shedding
- Drooling Potential
- Easy To Groom
- General Health
- Potential For Weight Gain
- Size

Trainability

- Easy To Train
- Intelligence
- Potential For Mouthiness
- Prey Drive
- Tendency To Bark Or Howl
- Wanderlust Potential

Physical Needs

- Energy Level
- Intensity
- Exercise Needs
- Potential For Playfulness

Vital Stats:

- Dog Breed Group: Companion Dogs
- Height: 8 to 9 inches tall at the shoulder
- Weight: 4 to 6 pounds
- Life Span: 12 to 15 years

BACKGROUND OF YORKSHIRE TERRIER BREEDING

Dogs that flushed out and killed rats in clothing mills in Northern England in the mid 18th century were useful little dogs. These dogs came to be known by that county where they were found and developed. The counties of Yorkshire and its adjoining county of Lancashire had many clothing mills that needed these small but feisty dogs. Small dogs from Scotland of the terrier type influenced the look and utility of the developing breed. The Paisley Terrier and the Maltese breed were part of the early profile of the breed. At first, the breed clubs did not differentiate among the various types of long-haired terrier-type dogs—all were labeled "Yorkshire terriers".

HUDDERSFIELD BEN

The differentiation of the breed as its own happened with the appearance of a famous show and stud dog named Huddersfield Ben. This dog is called the really first Yorkshire terrier, and the progenitor of the many that followed him. This dog was whelped in 1865. He was owned by Mary Ann Foster in Yorkshire, England.

Huddersfield Ben was the product of a mother-son pairing. The dog won 74 dog shows in its career. He sired many offspring in his short six years. Ben weighed about 9 pounds, but his offspring frequently weighed seven pounds or less. The memory of Ben was preserved both by a painting of him by George Earl and in the descendants he created. Huddersfield Ben has been called, the father of the breed.

RISE IN POPULARITY

The success of Huddersfield Ben as a show dog and the interest of small companion dogs for ladies and gentlemen of the Victorian era helped grow its initial popularity in England. The Kennel Club was founded in 1873, and the Yorkshire terrier was one of the first breed to be recognized (in 1874). The breed became a success in the United States as well, and the breed was recognized by the AKC in 1885.

In the United States, the breed took a dip in popularity in the late 1930s and early 1940s. However, the war exploits of a dog named Smoky helped bring back interest in the breed. According to the story, Smoky was found in a foxhole in New Guinea by a soldier who sold it to another soldier, Corporal William Wynne. The dog remained with Wynne throughout some harrowing ordeals of combat. The dog was credited with saving its owner's life by warning him of incoming shells. When Wynne and Smoky made it back home to Cleveland in 1945, a front-page story about the dog was featured in the Cleveland Press. This article brought fame to the breed, and soon Yorkie's were again being registered in great numbers.

RECENT DAYS

The arrival of the internet has been a big boom for Yorkie breeders. The size of the Yorkie makes it easy to transport them great distances, and their appealing look and size often go viral on social media. In the United States, an industry of breeders who market and sell dogs online has exploded. Some buyers, in fact, don't see the dog for real until it is picked up at the airport. Yorkies are a favorite breed of unscrupulous puppy mills. More dogs capable of being crammed into the same space means more money for these unethical breeders. The parent club in America has taken steps to educate the public about the problem. The Yorkshire Terrier Club of America maintains a list of breeders that have promised to behave ethically.

The popularity of the Yorkie ebbs and wanes in the United States. The Yorkshire terrier breed was listed the third most popular breed in 2010. The Yorkshire terrier's popularity has been declining somewhat with the rise in interest in larger dogs. In 2016, the Yorkshire terrier ranked 9th on the AKC list of most popular breeds. The breed has at times been featured at the sides of celebrities like Audrey Hepburn (1950), and more recently the first daughter, Ivanka Trump.

AKC standards of the Yorkshire terrier have largely gone unchanged since its beginning. The perky little terrier is a long-haired dog that does not exceed 7 pounds. It has a small head, alert eyes, and has four allowed colors combinations (black and tan, black and gold, blue and tan, blue and gold). The head and feet should be all tan, the body a dark blue, and all colors should exclude interspersed black color. Solid colors and any white markings (except a smidge on the chest) are disqualifications. According to AKC standards, the tail should be docked. The Kennel Club because of legal requirements allows docked and undocked tails.

MORE ABOUT THIS BREED

The Yorkshire Terrier, nicknamed the Yorkie, seems quite full of himself, and why not? With his long silky coat and perky topknot, the Yorkshire Terrier is one of the most glamorous representatives of the dog world, sure to attract attention wherever he goes. Because he's so small he often travels in style — in special dog purses toted around by his adoring owner.

The long steel-blue and tan coat may be the Yorkie's crowning glory, but it's his personality that truly endears him to his family. Oblivious to his small size (weighing in at no more than seven pounds), the Yorkshire Terrier is a big dog in a small body, always on the lookout for adventure and maybe even a bit of trouble.

Yorkshire Terriers are affectionate towards their people as one would expect from a companion dog, but true to their terrier heritage, they're sometimes suspicious of strangers, and will bark at strange sounds and intruders. In consideration of your neighbors, it's important to tone down their yappiness and teach them when and when not to bark.

They also can bc aggrcssivc toward strangc dogs, and no squirrel is safe from them.

Despite their bravado, Yorkshire Terriers have a soft side too. They need lots of attention and time with their family. Long hours of being left alone is not for them. It's not a good idea to over-protect your Yorkie, however; they'll pick up on your feelings very quickly, and if your actions say the world's a dangerous place for them, they can become neurotic.

Because of their size, Yorkshire Terriers do better with older children who've been taught to respect them than with toddlers and small children. They can become snappish if they're startled or teased.

As long as they get some exercise every day — perhaps a good play session in the living room or a nice walk around the block — Yorkies make fine apartment dogs.

No matter what home they live in, they'll get along with other resident dogs and cats — so long as they were raised with them. Yorkies may become possessive of their owners if a new pet is brought into the house. Being terriers, they may want to challenge the "intruder," and if a fight breaks out, the terrier spirit is to fight to the death. Take a lot of care when you're introducing a Yorkie to a new animal.

A glamorous coat, small size, spunky personality, and undying loyalty to his people. Is it any wonder that Yorkshire Terriers are the second most popular dog breed in the U.S. today?

Highlights

- Yorkshire Terriers are known for being difficult to housetrain. Crate-training is recommended.
- Yorkshire Terriers don't like the cold and are prone to chills, especially if they're damp or in damp areas.
- Because of their small size, delicate structure, and terrier personality, Yorkshire Terrier generally aren't recommended for households with toddlers or small children.
- Some Yorkshire Terriers can be "yappy," barking at every sound they hear. Early and consistent training can help. If you don't feel qualified to provide this training, consult a professional dog trainer.
- Yorkshire Terriers can have delicate digestive systems and may be picky eaters. Eating problems can occur if your Yorkie has teeth or gum problems as well. If your Yorkie is showing discomfort when eating or after eating, take him to the vet for a checkup.
- Yorkshire Terriers think they are big dogs and will try to pick a fight with a big dog if allowed. Be sure

to keep your Yorkie under control. Even better, try to socialize your Yorkie at an early age by taking him to obedience classes.

- Yorkies tend to retain their puppy teeth, especially the canines. When your puppy is around five months old, check his teeth often. If you notice that an adult tooth is trying to come in but the baby tooth is still there, take him to your vet. Retained baby teeth can cause the adult teeth to come in unevenly, which may contribute to tooth decay in later years.
- To get a healthy dog, never buy a puppy from an irresponsible breeder, puppy mill, or pet store. Look for a reputable breeder who tests her breeding dogs to make sure they're free of genetic diseases that they might pass onto the puppies, and that they have sound temperaments.

History

During the Industrial Revolution in England, Scottish workers came to Yorkshire to work in the coal mines, textile mills, and factories, bringing with them a dog known as a Clydesdale Terrier or Paisley Terrier. These dogs were much larger than the Yorkshire Terrier we know today, and it's thought that they were used primarily to catch rats in the mills.

The Clydesdale Terriers were probably crossed with other types of terrier, perhaps the English Black and Tan Toy Terrier and the Skye Terrier. The Waterside Terrier may also have contributed to the development of the Yorkshire Terrier. This was a small dog with a long blue-gray coat.

In 1861, a Yorkshire Terrier was shown in a bench show as a "broken-haired Scotch Terrier." A dog named Huddersfield Ben, born in 1865, became a popular show dog and is considered to be the father of the modern Yorkshire Terrier. The breed acquired that name in 1870 because that's where most of its development had taken place.

Yorkshire Terriers were first registered in the British Kennel Club stud book in 1874. The first Yorkshire Terrier breed club in England was formed in 1898.

The earliest record of a Yorkshire Terrier being born in the U.S. was in 1872. Yorkshire Terriers were able to compete in dog shows as early as 1878. In those early shows,

Yorkshire Terriers classes were divided by weight — under 5 pounds and 5 pounds and over. Eventually, exhibitors settled on one class with an average of between 3 and 7 pounds.

Size

Yorkshire Terriers should be 8 to 9 inches at the shoulder and weigh no more than seven pounds, with four to six pounds being preferred.

Yorkies are inconsistent in size. It's not unusual for a single litter to contain one Yorkie weighing less than four pounds, one who weighs five or six pounds, and one who grows to be 12 to 15 pounds.

Beware of breeders who offer "tea cup" Yorkshire Terriers. Dogs who are smaller than the standard are prone to genetic disorders and are at a higher health risk in general.

Personality

Smart and self-assured, the Yorkshire Terrier is a combination of endearingly small size and adventurous terrier spirit. The breed displays a range of personalities. Some are cuddly and perky, wanting nothing more than to follow in their people's footsteps throughout the day. Others are mischievous, outgoing, and into everything.

Set limits, and your Yorkie will be a wonderful companion, but if you spoil him, watch out! Start training when they're puppies, and you'll have much better luck than if you let them have their way and then try to correct bad habits.

Like all dogs, Yorkies needs early socialization — exposure to many different people, sights, sounds, and experiences — when they're young. Socialization helps ensure that your Yorkie will be a friendly, well-rounded dog.

Health

Yorkies are generally healthy, but like all breeds, they're prone to certain health conditions.

If you're buying a puppy, find a good breeder who will show you health clearances for both your puppy's parents. Health clearances prove that a dog has been tested for and cleared of a particular condition. In Yorkies, you should expect to see health clearances from the Orthopedic Foundation for Animals (OFA) for hip dysplasia (with a score of fair or better), elbow dysplasia, hypothyroidism, and von Willebrand's disease; from Auburn University for thrombopathia; and from the Canine Eye Registry Foundation (CERF) certifying that eyes are normal. You can confirm health clearances by checking the OFA web site (offa.org).

Patellar Luxation

Also known as "slipped stifles," this is a common problem in small dogs. It is caused when the patella, which has three parts — the femur (thigh bone), patella (knee cap), and tibia (calf) — is not properly lined up. This causes a lameness in the leg or an abnormal gait in the dog. It is a disease that is present at birth although the actual misalignment or luxation does not always occur until much later. The rubbing caused by patellar luxation can lead to arthritis, which is a degenerative joint disease. There are four grades of Patellar Luxation ranging from grade I, which is an occasional luxation causing temporary lameness in the joint, to grade IV, in which the turning of the tibia is severe and the patella cannot be realigned manually. This gives the dog a bowlegged appearance. Severe grades of patellar luxation may require surgical repair.

Progressive Retinal Atrophy (PRA)

A degenerative eye disorder. Blindness caused by PRA is a slow process resulting from the loss of photoreceptors at the back of the eye. PRA is detectable years before the dog shows any signs of blindness. Reputable breeders have their dogs' eyes certified annually by a veterinary ophthalmologist.

Portosystemic Shunt

Portosystemic shunt (PSS) is an abnormal flow of blood between the liver and the body. That's a problem, because the liver is responsible for detoxifying the body, metabolizing nutrients, and eliminating drugs. Signs can include but are not limited to neurobehavioral abnormalities, lack of appetite, hypoglycemia (low blood sugar), intermittent gastrointestinal issues, urinary tract problems, drug intolerance, and stunted growth. Signs usually appear before two years of age. Corrective surgery can be helpful in long-term management, as can a special diet.

Hypoglycemia

Like many toy and small breed dogs, Yorkies can suffer from hypoglycemia when stressed, especially when they are puppies. Hypoglycemia is caused by low blood sugar. Some of the signs may include weakness, confusion, a wobbly gait, and seizure-like episodes. If your dog is susceptible to this, talk to your vet about prevention and treatment options.

Collapsed trachea

The trachea, which carries air to the lungs, tends to collapse easily. The most common sign of a collapsed trachea is a chronic, dry, harsh cough that many describe as being similar to a "goose honk." Collapsed trachea can be treated medically or surgically.

Reverse sneezing

This condition is sometimes confused with a collapsed trachea. This is a far less serious condition and lasts only a few minutes. Reverse sneezing primarily occurs when your dog is excited or tries to eat or drink too fast. It also can occur when there are pollens or other irritants in the air. Secretions from the dog's nose drop onto their soft palate, causing it to close over the windpipe in an automatic reaction. This can be very frightening to your Yorkie, but as soon as he calms down, the reverse sneezing stops. Gently stroke his throat to help him relax.

Eye infections, teeth, and gum problems also can occur.

Care

Yorkshire Terriers enjoy taking a walk with you or playing outside, but since they're very active while indoors, it doesn't take a lot of effort to keep them well exercised.

In general, Yorkies are receptive to training, especially if it brings them attention for performing cute tricks or performing in agility or obedience trials. They can be difficult to housetrain, however, because their "accidents" are so small and easy to clean up that people let it slide. That's a mistake. It's better to show them where to go from the beginning and reward them for doing their business in the right place. When you make the effort, you can end up with a very well trained Yorkie indeed.

They definitely are housedogs and don't tolerate extreme heat or cold well. Many people paper train their Yorkshire Terriers so they don't have to take them outdoors when the weather is too hot or cold.

Yorkies love squeaky toys, but it's important to check the toy every few days to make sure they haven't chewed them open and pulled out the squeaker. They especially enjoy fetching toys that you throw for them. If you're crafty, consider crocheting a ball for your Yorkie — larger than a golf ball but smaller than a tennis ball — and stuffing it with used panty hose. He'll love it!

Feeding

Recommended daily amount: 1/2 to 3/4 cup of high-quality dry food a day, divided into two meals.

Note: How much your adult dog eats depends on his size, age, build, metabolism, and activity level. Dogs are individuals, just like people, and they don't all need the same amount of food. It almost goes without saying that a highly active dog will need more than a couch potato dog. The quality of dog food you buy also makes a difference — the better the dog food, the further it will go toward nourishing your dog and the less of it you'll need to shake into your dog's bowl.

Take care that your Yorkie doesn't get fat. Roly-poly is not a good look for this elegant breed. Keep your Yorkie in good shape by measuring his food and feeding him twice a day rather than leaving food out all the time. If you're unsure whether he's overweight, give him the eye test and the hands-on test.

First, look down at him. You should be able to see a waist. Then place your hands on his back, thumbs along the spine, with the fingers spread downward. You should be able to feel but not see his ribs without having to press hard. If you can't, he needs less food and more exercise.

Coat Color And Grooming

The Yorkshire Terrier's coat is long, silky, and perfectly straight without any hint of a wave. Show dogs have hair that reaches the floor. They have a single coat and shed very little.

Puppies are born black, with the blue and tan coat developing gradually, usually after they're a year old. Puppies that start to lightcn bcforc thcy'rc a ycar old oftcn turn gray rather than blue.

From the back of the head to the tip of the tail, the hair is a dark steel-blue — sometimes described as the blue of a rifle barrel — with a bluish sheen when seen in the sunlight. The head is bright gold, not reddish, with tan hairs that are darker at the roots than at the ends. The headfall (the hair that falls over the face) is long with the same golden hue as the face.

The hair is slightly darker at the base of the ears and on the muzzle. The tan on the head doesn't extend past the ears, and no black hairs are mixed in with the tan. Yorkshire Terriers have tan legs as well, but the tan color doesn't extend above the elbow.

An interesting fact is that Yorkies tend to become lighter with age. Hormonal changes can also affect color. Females in heat go lighter, and then darken again after their season is over.

Grooming a long-haired Yorkshire Terrier is not for the faint of heart, especially if he has a "soft" coat that tangles easily instead of a silky one! Even if you keep his coat trimmed short, gently brush your Yorkie's coat every day to help prevent mats and keep him clean.

Small breeds are prone to dental problems, and Yorkies are no exception. Yorkshire Terriers tend to form a lot of tartar on their teeth and can lose their teeth at a young age, so brush their teeth regularly and schedule a professional cleaning by your vet at least once a year.

As part of the grooming process, check your Yorkie's ears regularly. Look inside them and give them a good sniff. If they appear to be infected (have an offensive odor, redness, or a brown discharge), ask your vet to check them. If there's hair in the ear canal, pluck it out with your fingers or ask your vet or groomer to do it for you.

Bathe your Yorkie weekly to keep his coat beautiful and shiny. There's no need to rub the coat to wash it. After wetting the coat and applying the shampoo, all you need to do is run your fingers through it to lift the dirt out. Apply conditioner, then rinse thoroughly.

When you're drying your Yorkie, spray the coat with a light conditioner. Give the coat a spritz with a light conditioner when you're brushing him as well. Never brush a dry or dirty coat or you'll break the hair.

Trim your Yorkie's nails after each bath to prevent painful tears and other problems. If you hear them clicking on the floor, they're too long. Dog toenails have blood vessels in them, and if you cut too far you can cause bleeding — and your dog may not cooperate the next time he sees the nail clippers come out. So, if you're not experienced trimming dog nails, ask a vet or groomer for pointers.

When you're grooming your Yorkie, be sure to check the anal area and trim around it with scissors if the hair's getting too long. Usually trimming about a half inch of hair around it is enough.

After you've brushed your Yorkie and he's dry, collect the hair on the top of his head, starting at the outer corner of the eye, going back at an angle toward the center of head, then back down to the outer corner of the other eye. Brush this hair up and fasten it with a latex band, and then add your favorite bow.

Begin accustoming your Yorkie to being brushed and examined when he's a puppy. Handle his paws frequently — dogs are touchy about their feet — and look inside his mouth. Make grooming a positive experience filled with praise and rewards, and you'll lay the groundwork for easy veterinary exams and other handling when he's an adult.

As you groom, check for sores, rashes, or signs of infection such as redness, tenderness, or inflammation on the skin, in the nose, mouth, and eyes, and on the feet. Eyes should be clear, with no redness or discharge. Your careful weekly exam will help you spot potential health problems early.

Feeding

How much, when and what to feed your Yorkshire terrier?

HOW MUCH AND WHEN TO FEED YOUR YORKIE!

The amount of food and the feeding times will depend on the how old your Yorkie is and your his activity level.

At about 3 months old

A puppy needs to be free-fed. This means you leave food available to your puppy at all times. This helps to prevent hypoglycemia (low blood sugar) which is prone in small breeds, and allows the pup to eat as needed which is important because your puppy is going through a growth stage.

At 3 months - 6 months

It is important to set schedules meals. This is because you will be housebreaking at this age, also when your puppy has a well scheduled day his behavior will be better. It is recommended that you feed your puppy 3-4 meals per day. Morning, lunchtime, early evening and 2 hours before bed time (if feeding a fourth meal). The last meal should give you time to take your puppy out to potty before bed. Your puppy will be eating more now than when he is an adult. So each meal should be between 1/4 and 1/2 cup of food, but to accurately determine how much your puppy will eat allow your pup to eat for 15 minutes and then take away the food. Pups vary so much following a strict guideline of how much to feed can leave them underfed or overfed neither of which is good especial for a puppy.

6 months to 1 year

Start working your way down from 3 or 4 meals a day to just 1or 2 meal per day. Some owners choose to feed three, however this means 3 bowel movements you need to account for. But also keep in mind that because of a Yorkshire terrier's small size they do get hypoglycemia (low blood sugar).

WHAT TO FEED YOUR YORKIE!

MEALS

Give them a top-of-the-line dry food. What is top-of-the line? Read the ingredients! Check that they are USDA inspected and not packed with a lot of fillers, such as corn. The top ingredient should be meat, not a meat by-product. You can also add things like cooked vegetables (green beans, carrots and peas are best. Even canned pumpkin is okay as long as its unsweetened and in small amounts because it's a natural laxative). Other things that you can add are brown rice, whole grain pasta and cooked meats. Raw meat isn't recommended because of bacteria.

TREATS

Pick treats come fortified with vitamins and minerals that promote clean teeth and fresher breath. This is especially important for Yorkies, as they easily develop dental problems. Be sure you always buy small treats for Yorkies, they are a small dog. You can also always make healthy treats for your Yorkie as long as you use high quality ingredients.

CHILDREN AND OTHER PETS

Because of their small size, Yorkies aren't suited to families with young children. Most breeders won't sell puppies to people whose children are younger than 5 or 6 years old. It's just too easy for children to drop them, step on them, or hold them too tightly.

Yorkies can get along well with other pets, including cats, if socialized to them at an early age. They're bold in going after strange dogs, however, even those that outweigh them by a factor of ten, and protecting them from themselves becomes second nature to people with Yorkies.

RESCUE GROUPS

Yorkshire Terriers are often purchased without any clear understanding of what goes into owning one. There are many Yorkies in need of adoption and or fostering. There are a number of rescues that we have not listed. If you don't see a rescue listed for your area, contact the national breed club or a local breed club and they can point you toward a Yorkie rescue.

- Rescue Me Yorkie Rescue
- United Yorkie Rescue
- Yorkshire Terrier National Rescue Inc.
- YTCA Rescue, Inc.

DO YORKIES HAVE HYPOALLERGENIC COATS?

One of the popular selling points is that the breed is somewhat hypoallergenic. Yorkies have a silky coat that resembles human hair. It lacks the undercoat typical of other breeds. The breed only lightly sheds. However, people allergic to dogs are not always allergic to the fur itself. Many allergic reactions are due to the skin or dander of the dog. A dog that sheds little has less dander, but less is not the same thing as none. For highly allergic individuals a little is too much. Some people have allergies to the saliva of the dog.

Yorkies do not make the list of breeds recommended by the AKC for the ten percent of the population that suffers from dog allergies. The Maltese do, though. So is the Poodle. The Maltese is thought to be one of the breeds that were early on incorporated into the gene pool. The coats of the two are very similar. It is likely, therefore, that the low-shedding Yorkie would be tolerated well by someone with less severe dog allergies.

HOW BIG ARE YORKSHIRE TERRIERS?

According to their national breed club, Yorkies should be about 7-8 inches at the shoulder and weigh 3-7 lbs. But some individuals are smaller, and many are quite a bit larger.

Let me ask you: Have you heard of a Teacup Yorkie? a Tiny Toy Yorkie? an Extreme Tiny Yorkie?

Those phrases are made-up. There is no such breed or variety as a Teacup Yorkie, Tiny Toy Yorkie, or Extreme Tiny Yorkie. Those are simply cutesy marketing terms that some clever breeders use to try to make you think you're getting some kind of extra-special Yorkshire Terrier.

Such a breeder might tell you that "Toy" Yorkies are a certain weight range, "Tiny Toy" Yorkies are slightly smaller, "Extreme Tiny" Yorkies are smaller than that, etc. These breeders might even price their dogs according to weight, as if that alone should define a dog's value. And their prices are usually outrageous.

It's all hogwash.

There is only one Yorkshire Terrier breed. Period. And no matter what his size, he is considered a Toy breed. Whether an individual weighs 2 pounds or 6 pounds or 12 pounds, he's still just a Yorkshire Terrier, which is a Toy breed.

Unfortunately, Yorkies under 3 or 4 pounds are greater risks when it comes to health. Their bones are more fragile. There isn't enough room in their mouth for healthy teeth. Their internal organs are often weak and can fail suddenly. They tend to have difficulty regulating their blood sugar and can go into hypoglycemic shock if they go too long without eating.

Responsible Yorkshire Terrier breeders never try to produce these high-risk creatures. If a tiny Yorkie pops up in one of their normal-size litters, they find the best home they can for it. But they try not to produce them in the first place.

How can you tell whether a Yorkshire Terrier puppy will mature at 4 pounds and up? There's a rule of thumb that says a puppy will most likely mature at 4 pounds and up if he already weighs at least 2 pounds at 10-12 weeks old. It's not perfect, but it's usually pretty close.

ARE THERE DIFFERENT "TYPES" OF YORKSHIRE TERRIERS?

The short answer is No, there's only the one breed. Some people think a "Teacup" Yorkie is a different kind of Yorkshire Terrier. Not true. See the Size section just above this one. That section should answer your questions about the different sizes of Yorkies.But certainly the different sizes can look different. For example, a 3-pounder looks quite delicate, compared to a sturdy 8-pounder.

Grooming can also make one Yorkshire Terrier look different from another. If you've been to a dog show or seen one on TV, you'll see that those Yorkies with their flowing coats look different from, say, your neighbor's clipped-short Yorkie.

Show dog coats are sculpted just so, to win ribbons. But those styles are woefully impractical for a family companion. Many show dogs have to be carried everywhere or confined to crates or concrete kennel runs so they don't get messy playing in the back yard.Or else the breeder pins up all the hair with curlers, rubber bands, and barrettes. I love Yorkies, but I don't like to see them like that. It just looks.... wrong.

HOW MUCH EXERCISE DO YORKSHIRE TERRIERS NEED?

In theory, Yorkies can get most of their exercise indoors. The problem is that a Yorkshire Terrier can become too hyped-up if they're forced to exercise entirely by running around the house.In my Respect Training book for puppies, I explain why you should always encourage calmness indoors. A dog who dashes around, jumping and barking, is keeping himself in an excitable, over-stimulated state of mind. That isn't psychologically healthy and usually leads to behavior problems.

So try to take your Yorkshire Terrier outside. You can keep a Yorkie in an apartment with no yard. But he'll be much happier with a fenced yard, however small, where he can stretch his legs and run around.

ARE YORKSHIRE TERRIERS EASY TO TRAIN?

Most Yorkies are bright and quick to learn, though that often depends on what you're trying to teach them. They tend to learn tricks readily: Beg, Dance, Spin, Roll Over. Of course they expect a treat after they perform. They can be little divas!

It's more challenging to teach a Yorkie to walk properly on a leash. They can be very opinionated, so they dislike the leash "telling them what to do" and may dart this way and that, or refuse to walk at all.

The two main behavior problems in Yorkies:

Housebreaking

As a behavioral consultant, I would put the Yorkshire Terrier on my Top 5 List of Hardest Breeds to Housebreak.

If you live in a cold or rainy climate, it's worse, because Yorkies hate both the cold and the rain.

Barking

With their keen senses, Yorkies make excellent watchdogs. However, this can make them too quick to sound the alarm at every new sight and sound. You have to be equally quick to stop them before excessive barking becomes an established habit.

HOW SOCIABLE ARE YORKSHIRE TERRIERS?

Are they friendly with strangers?

Keen of eye and sharp of tongue, most Yorkshire Terriers are very quick to announce strangers at the door. Once the visitor comes in, some Yorkies will be friendly and outgoing. But many others have the standoffish or suspicious nature of a true terrier.

Unfortunately, suspicious dogs can morph into shrill dogs who won't stop barking. And shrill dogs can easily turn nasty. You must teach a Yorkshire Terrier that he doesn't need to like strangers, but he does need to accept them politely.

Are Yorkshire Terriers good with children?

A better question is rather, "Are Yorkies SAFE with children?" My answer is, "With most children under about the age of 9 or 10.... no."

A child can seriously injure a Yorkshire Terrier by stepping on him, or by sitting on him when he's curled under a blanket or pillow, where he frequently likes to sleep.

In addition, many Yorkies feel overwhelmed by the loud voices, roughhousing, and quick movements that children can't help making – and stress and fearfulness (even defensive biting) may be the result. Safety is especially an issue with the smallest Yorkies. Larger individuals are sturdier.

ARE YORKSHIRE TERRIERS GOOD WITH OTHER PETS?

In your own household, yes. Most Yorkies are great with other dogs and cats in your family. But I don't recommend keeping the tinier Yorkies in a home with large dogs. A toy dog can be injured simply by a larger dog jumping around with enthusiasm and accidentally landing on the smaller one.

With strange dogs, Yorkies are surprisingly bossy and scrappy. If you're out for a walk and your Yorkie spies another dog, he might begin barking and lunging. The bigger the dog, the more demonstrative the Yorkie seems to become.

GROOMING: DO YORKSHIRE TERRIERS SHED? ARE THEY EASY TO GROOM?

Great news! Yorkshire Terriers shed very little, produce very little dander, and are one of the best breeds for allergy sufferers.

The bad news.... without frequent brushing and combing, Yorkshire Terriers become a matted mess. Mats and tangles are painful. When hairs fuse together, they pull on the dog's skin whenever he walks. Especially look for mats behind the ears, under the arms, and on the stomach. In longhaired dogs, I always clip the groin (and anal area) short so it stays clean and sanitary when the dog goes to the bathroom.

If you can't commit to the brushing, you have to commit to frequent trimming to keep the coat short, neat, and healthy.

For the easiest maintenance, you can shear the coat very short with clippers. Then you won't need to brush it at all.

Personally, I love this sheared cut. It's so easy to care for, so comfortable for the dog, and makes a Yorkshire Terrier look like a cute puppy throughout his life!

ARE YORKSHIRE TERRIERS HEALTHY? HOW LONG DO THEY LIVE?

Like most toy breeds, Yorkshire Terriers are usually long-lived, with a typical lifespan of 12-15 years. And as with most toy breeds, the leading health problem in Yorkies is injury. Leg fractures from falling or jumping off things or being stepped on. Choking on something tiny they find on the floor. Being overdosed with something toxic, even a medication or flea powder. Being attacked or jumped on by a larger dog.... the list goes on.

As far as diseases go....Liver shunt is a very serious problem in Yorkshire Terriers. At one veterinary university, a full one-third of their liver shunt patients are Yorkies.

Expensive surgery may also be required for

- dental disease – a problem in all toy breeds

- a weak/defective windpipe (collapsing trachea) that causes chronic severe coughing that sounds like a goose honking
- loose knee joints (luxating patella) that cause lameness and pain; Yorkshire Terriers have the 2nd highest rate of luxating patella of all breeds, with nearly 1 in 4 Yorkies affected

Eye diseases are also worrisome; lots of Yorkies are blind from cataracts.

WHAT COLORS DO YORKSHIRE TERRIERS COME IN?

The official Yorkshire Terrier clubs, along with breeders who show Yorkies in the conformation ring, assert that the ONLY correct colors are tan or gold, with a blue saddle.

Blue?? Yes, it looks more like gray, but in the canine world, blue is the term that is used. In Yorkies, the blue is supposed to be dark steel blue, but is often more silvery blue.

Yorkies do come in other colors (deemed "incorrect" by their national club):

- Tan or gold with a black saddle. Like all Yorkies, these dogs were born black and tan, but then the black never changed over to blue. This color hearkens back to the Yorkshire Terrier's English ancestors from the 1800s – working terriers who were often black and tan.
- Solid tan or gold. Very little, if any, blue saddle.
- Liver or chocolate (brown). These Yorkies have inherited a color-modifying gene that changes their blue/gray pigment to brown (any shade from light to chocolate). All blue pigment is affected, including their nose and the pads of their feet.
- Particolor. White with colored patches.

There is even a tricolored "spin-off" breed called the Biewer (pronounced Beaver) Terrier. Created in Germany in the 1980s, a Biewer is essentially a tricolor Yorkie, with the colors needing to appear in a very specific pattern.

Unfortunately, from a genetic standpoint, creating dogs with an emphasis on "perfect" markings is never a good thing. You end up with a limited, non-diverse gene pool. Also, focusing on something as trivial as color usually leads to problems with health and temperament down the line. Currently Biewers are being marketed for pretty high prices.

AN IMPORTANT NOTE ABOUT COLOR IN YORKSHIRE TERRIERS

The most distinctive characteristic of an adult Yorkshire Terrier is its long blue and tan silk coat. A puppy is born black and tan, but the only recognized colors for adults when registering with AKC are blue and gold, blue and tan, black and gold, or black and tan.

The AKC Breed Standard and YTCA Code of Ethics do not recognize any other color dogs than noted above. This includes all gold, born blue, liver (also known as red or chocolate), and parti-colors. One of the reasons for avoiding breeding "off-colored" Yorkies is because it could be a genetic defect that may affect the dog's health. Some health problems can include, but aren't limited to, severe skin problems, allergies, total hair loss and in some cases long-term illness and/or death.

A responsible breeder will not intentionally breed for undesirable traits.On very rare occasions, a breeder will have a puppy born with a color anomaly. That puppy should undergo careful health screenings before being placed in a spay/neuter (non breeding) home. A breeder should certainly never promote these deviations as being desirable or rare.

There are many issues that potential Yorkie owners need to study before purchasing their dog. We hope you will read the helpful information at this web site and make an informed decision. It could very possibly save you aggravation, disappointment and expense. We wish you the best of luck in your pursuit of a happy, healthy Yorkshire Terrier.

HOW DO I ADOPT A YORKSHIRE TERRIER?

Yorkies are often available from dog rescue groups. Some also show up at animal shelters, though these are usually snapped up quickly because so many prospective owners are seeking a tiny dog. A Yorkshire Terrier might be turned over to a rescue group or shelter because of housebreaking issues or barking. But Yorkies are often owned by elderly people, and when elderly people pass away, if no one in the family is willing to take the dog, he gets abandoned, even if he has no behavior issues at all.

WHAT BREEDS ARE SIMILAR TO YORKSHIRE TERRIERS?

The Silky Terrier looks like a largish (8-12 pounds) Yorkshire Terrier. Compared to Yorkies, Silkys tend to be more stable in temperament, but also more terrier-ish – more independent and hardier. Silkys are fine for some allergy-sufferers, but perhaps not as tried-and-true as a Yorkie.

If your heart is set on a tiny dog and you're allergic, the light-shedding Maltese also fits the bill. Compared to Yorkshire Terriers, Maltese have a softer, sweeter temperament, as their ancestry is not terrier, but spaniel.

The Toy Poodle is the most hypo-allergenic of all coated breeds. Compared to a Yorkie, the Toy Poodle has a softer, sweeter temperament, is very quick to learn, and is easier to housebreak. The trade-off is more grooming.

If you would prefer a spunkier little guy with a low-maintenance coat, and you don't mind some shedding, consider the Toy Fox Terrier. He's similar to a Yorkie and a Silky in being a blend of toy and terrier traits.

WHAT TO EXPECT WHEN CARING FOR A YORKSHIRE TERRIER

Owning a dog is not just a privilege; it's a responsibility. They depend on us for, at minimum, food and shelter, and deserve much more. When you take a dog into your life, you need to understand the commitment that dog ownership entails.

Health

Yorkshire Terriers are generally healthy dogs, and responsible breeders screen their stock for health conditions such as eye anomalies and luxating patella, a dislocated kneecap once called a 'trick knee' in humans. To help avoid the latter, care should be taken to limit the Yorkie's jumping height, especially as a puppy.

Recommended Health Tests From the National Breed Club:

- Patella Evaluation
- Ophthalmologist Evaluation

Grooming

The Yorkshire Terrier's coat is very similar to human hair and should be treated accordingly. If the coat is kept long, it needs to be brushed daily. To avoid eye irritation, the hair on the upper part of the head should be trimmed short or pulled up into a topknot. The Yorkie will need a bath every week or so. Check the ears weekly for any debris or signs of infection. The breed's national parent club, the Yorkshire Terrier Club of America, provides detailed grooming and bathing instructions on its website.

Exercise

Even small dogs require exercise to stay healthy, both mentally and physically. Yorkies will benefit from both moderate exercise, such as walks with their owner at a steady pace, as well as occasional short bursts of activity, such as chasing after a tennis ball in the backyard. A short walk twice a day will likely be enough for your Yorkie to see new scenery and burn off energy. Participating in dog sports such as obedience or agility also will provide beneficial activity to keep him healthy, while challenging his mind as well.

Training

Yorkies love their owners, and are very intelligent and eager to please. Offering effusive praise and treats for good behavior will work far better with the Yorkie than harsh corrections. Starting from an early age, the Yorkie should be socialized to strange situations, people, and other dogs. Take him into new situations slowly, and always in a calm and happy atmosphere. These should be positive experiences. Despite their small size, Yorkies can participate in and excel at canine activities such as rally, agility and obedience, and many Yorkies serve with their human partners in roles such as therapy work.

Nutrition

The Yorkshire Terrier should do well on a high-quality dog food, whether commercially manufactured or home-prepared with your veterinarian's supervision and approval. Any diet should be appropriate to the dog's age (puppy, adult, or senior). Some dogs are prone to getting overweight, so watch your dog's calorie consumption and weight level. Treats can be an important aid in training, but giving too many can cause obesity. Learn about which human foods arc safc for dogs, and which are not. Check with your vet if you have any concerns about your dog's weight or diet. Clean, fresh water should be available at all times.

CHAPTER TWO

BREEDING BASICS

Breeding any small breed dog requires a wealth of knowledge. The information provided here is the basics of breeding and overview of the breeding process. Before you begin breeding you should see a vet and registered breeder to learn more.

Before Breeding

Start by making sure you know the Yorkshire terrier breed inside and out. Read, study and join clubs. Now that you know this you can determine if you should or should not breed.

Step one in determining whether you should breed is finding a female Yorkshire terrier of show dog quality, and then determine if she is healthy enough and old enough to be bred. Yorkies should be breed only between 2 and 5 years of age. They are also prone to a number of genetic conditions, so having your vet evaluate your female to make sure she is free of any genetic defects before breeding is of the highest priority.

Now that you have an acceptable female you will need to select a male that is compatible with her. Yorkies can vary in size, and choosing a male that is the same size or 1-2 pounds smaller than your female can help eliminate problems during delivery. The male you choose will also need to be checked by a vet to make sure he is free of any genetic or transmittable diseases. This is especial important if you are choosing a stud male (this is a male that you yourself do not own and are paying some kind of fee for). Be sure that these records are up to date.

Breeding

A Yorkie's breeding age should be two years old for both the males and the females. This way they are fully mature and genetic problems will be known. If you breed them younger than two the genetic problems may not have emerged yet.

Female Yorkies can experience problems with natural delivery due to their size, so it is recommended that you only breed them twice per year.

Now that you have a suitable female and male you must first start by evaluate your female's heat cycle. Your female will be receptive to breeding ten to fourteen days into her heat cycle. You may choose to breed outside this time, but this is the optimal period to breed.

Next you will need to place your female and male together and allow them time to get familiar with each other. You may want to do this before she is in heat to be sure that dogs get along and will not hurt each other when the time comes.

Now that they are familiar you may place them together for breeding. They will sniff and examine each other, and the male is likely to smell and lick the female's hindquarters. If she is receptive to him, he will mount her and they will "tie" for a period of time. The dogs may try and separate themselves during the tie, so be watchful that they do not injure themselves.

With-in 72 hours of the breeding taking place you should take your female to the vet for an evaluation of the breeding. The vet will need to monitor your female throughout her pregnancy to keep track of how many puppies she's having and how the pups are growing. This is especially important in small breeds like the Yorkie. Be sure that you always transport your Yorkie in her crate to keep her safe and comfortable. Remember she is pregnant and will need extra care.

Watch your female carefully as her due date approaches. Normal dog gestation is sixty-three days, so plan accordingly. Prepare your whelping area a week before your female is due. You will need a small whelping box with a heating pad and clean blankets for the puppies. A heating pad is vital, because Yorkies are small and need to be kept warm to thrive. Place the female in the whelping box throughout this week and allow her to make it comfortable so that she wants to give birth there. This will make you both more comfortable on the big day.

Have your regular vet's number and that of an emergancy vet on hand should you need them when your Yorkie starts to deliever.

Delivery

Watch your female carefully as her due date approaches. A Yorkies gestation is 63 days, so plan accordingly. Your female will begin nesting two or three days before giving birth. You can also take her temperature daily, making note of the reading. Within a day of giving birth, her temperature will drop by a few degrees.

Allow your female Yorkie to birth the puppies on her own, if she is able too. The labor should progress quickly, with puppies born every 20 to 30 minutes. If there is a delay of more than one hour, you need to call your vet immediately. Yorkies are very small, and a large puppy can get stuck in the birth canal, endangering the lives of your female and the other puppies. Therefor your vet might have to perform a caesarean section if the puppies are too large for your Yorkie to deliver on her own.

Monitor your female and her puppies after birth. They should begin nursing soon after being born and should be fairly active. Any lethargic puppies need to be seen by the vet as soon as posible. Keep the puppies warm, and do not handle them more than nessisary. Your female Yorkie needs time to recover and bond with her new babies.

HOW TO BREED YORKIES

If you plan to breed your Yorkshire terrier (Yorkie) there are some very important issues to consider long before you mate your dog. You need to evaluate the dog's suitability for breeding, its physical and breed characteristic traits, how the process of reproduction might effect the dog, and the potential pitfalls and complications of having a litter of pups. If you consider all of these issues before breeding your dog, and you still go through with it, your evaluation will prepare you better for the realities of the breeding process.

Deciding Whether to Breed Your Yorkie

Determine if your Yorkie is old enough to breed

A female Yorkie should not be used for breeding until she is 2 years old. A male Yorkie will generally have viable sperm when he is over a year old.

Assess whether your dog has the right physical traits for breeding

Does your dog have desirable breed traits? Does it meet breed standard minimums? According to the American Kennel Club a Yorkie should exhibit these traits:

- The Yorkie's body should be compact and well proportioned.
- In addition, a Yorkie's head should be "small and rather flat on top, the skull not too prominent or

round, the muzzle not too long, with the bite neither undershot nor overshot and teeth sound. Either scissors bite or level bite is acceptable. The nose is black. Eyes are medium in size and not too prominent; dark in color and sparkling with a sharp, intelligent expression. Eye rims are dark. Ears are small, V-shaped, carried erect and set not too far apart."

Assess whether your dog has the right temperament for breeding

It should appear confident but should be friendly towards people and not fearful. Fearfulness in dogs can be hereditary or a learned trait but you do not want to risk perpetuating a bad hereditary trait.

Determine whether you have the financial stability to breed your dog

A dog pregnancy could result in complications, which could cost you a lot of money. Possible complications to consider include an emergency C-section or serious medical conditions occurring in the mother. These can include hypocalcemia, metritis, or mastitis.

Are you prepared to raise any unsold puppies? All the puppies in any given litter do not always sell, so you need to be aware that you may be taking on a lifelong financial responsibility for a new puppy.

Be realistic about whether you have the time to devote to breeding your dog

Raising puppies is a full-time job. You will need time for daily handling and socializing the puppies, as only puppies that are socialized to humans make good pets.

The time spent playing and bonding with the puppies is in addition to the time it takes to care for them. Feeding and cleaning after puppies is no small job.

Contact a breeder to adopt a Yorkie that you can then breed

If you are looking to adopt a Yorkie you can breed, you should get the name of a well-respected breeder that has a good track record with successful offspring. Good breeders will encourage you to visit them, have good looking and social dogs and puppies, give the dogs plenty of room to roam, will only breed one type of dog, and will interview you about how you will raise the dog they bred.

- Contact local Yorkie clubs for a list of local breeders that do not run puppy mills.
- If there are no well-established breeders in your area, you may need to travel to get a dog that has all the positive breeding traits you want.
- When you are interacting with a well-regarded breeder, pay attention to how the person conducts business and how he or she interacts with the dogs. You can learn a lot just from watching how a professional conducts business.
- Make sure to assess all aspects of the breeding process. Use a checklist to make sure you have covered your bases, like the one provided by the Humane Society.

Breeding Yorkies

Understand the reproductive system of the male Yorkie

The external parts of the male Yorkie's reproductive system are the penis and the scrotum. The scrotum is a pouch that holds the dog's testicles. The sperm, which fertilize the female's egg, are produced in the testes.

Male dogs should ideally have two testes, which move from inside the body down into the scrotum during puberty. A mature male's testes are located outside the abdomen because the internal body temperature is too warm for sperm to grow normally. Because of this, dogs with undescended testes (testicles that do not move down into the scrotum) do not make good candidates to breed, as the problem can be inherited. They should be neutered because undescended testicles can cause health problems later.

Understand the reproductive system of the female Yorkie

Most of the female Yorkie's reproductive system is located inside her body. The only visible part is the vulva. Inside, the ovaries produce eggs and the female sex hormones estrogen and progesterone.

After eggs are fertilized by sperm, they attach to the uterine lining and grow into puppies.

Get a physical veterinary examination of both dogs

About one month before you breed your Yorkie it should be examined by a veterinarian. The vet should make sure the female is healthy enough to carry a pregnancy to term and that the male is free of diseases and physical problems.

Watch for signs that the female is physically ready to mate

Track the female's reproductive cycle so that you know when she will go into heat next. In general, a female dog generally goes into heat twice a year.

- The heat cycle starts with a preparatory stage, proestrus, when the vulva swells and a light bloody discharge occurs for 7-9 days. After this stage the bleeding slows down and the dog becomes receptive to breeding. This stage is called estrus or standing heat and is the most fertile time for breeding.
- Your veterinarian can determine if your dog is in heat by swabbing the inside of her vagina with a cotton swab. By examining the cells on the swab under a microscope the vet can determine if it is the right time for breeding.

Place the male and female together

When the female is physically ready to breed, she will bow to him and back into him. The male will usually reciprocate this interest and mount her for breeding. This process usually occurs naturally, without any outside intervention needed.

Advertise the puppies before they are born

You want to have people lined up who are going to adopt the puppies when they are born. The last thing you want is to be stuck with too many dogs.

- Advertise your puppies on local list-servs for Yorkie owners or with your local chapter of national dog organizations.
- Make a list of potential buyers. Since you won't know exactly how many puppies your dog will have, you need to basically make a waiting list. Let potential buyers know where they fall on the list, so that they know there is a chance they will not get a puppy in this litter.

Tips

- Talk to an experienced Yorkie breeder about his or her experiences with breeding. This can help you understand the realities of breeding and help you to determine if you want to take on this big responsibility.
- If you decide not to breed your dog you should have it desexed. This will help prevent unwanted puppies

in the future and it also lessens the risk of some health problems later in life.

HEALTH CONCERNS WHEN BREEDING YORKSHIRE TERRIERS

Yorkshire Terriers are affected by quite a few health conditions in comparison to other dog breeds. Generally, this is a direct consequence of their small size and a lot of inbreeding in a given dog's pedigree. When you decide to breed Yorkies, you must ensure their good health and sound genetics before attempting to organize a copulatory tie.

PERIODONTAL HEALTH

In general, toy breeds have dental problems because they have small mouths lacking sufficient room for all teeth to grow properly. The genetics of downsizing the palate and the teeth sometimes have not quite kept up with the rest of the dog.

Dogs have two sets of teeth—puppy and adult. The 28 puppy teeth (or deciduous teeth) come in at 3 weeks and the adult teeth start erupting at 3 months. Normally, the adult tooth replaces the puppy tooth. Usually, by four months all the puppy teeth are gone. By six months a dog should have all of its 42 adult teeth. If a puppy tooth is not pushed out, it will cause crowding of teeth in the dog's mouth. This crowding makes for a poor bite and is subject to tooth decay.

Yorkies will frequently retain some puppy teeth. The solution is to pull the baby tooth. All Yorkies should be given regular teeth cleanings to prevent gum disease and tooth decay. When breeding Yorkshire terriers, the breeder must have a schedule planned up with the vet for the year coming.

COMMON GENETIC DEFECTS

Progressive Retinal Atrophy is a genetic condition that crops up in Yorkies. In this condition, the rods and cones of in the dog's eyes deteriorate. The first signs are night blindness. This disease usually begins in middle aged dogs. There is no cure. Dogs with it will ultimately be blind. The Orthopedic Foundation for Animals recommends genetic testing and eye examination for dogs PRA is caused by recessive genes. There is a genetic test for it.

Yorkies are known for the strange goose-like honk they make when exposed to wind, exercise, or allergens. This sound results from the design of the windpipe (trachea) in the toy breed. It is a symptom of a serious condition called tracheal collapse. In this condition, the rings of cartilage that make up the trachea begin to collapse. Of course, obstruction of the airway for the dog can become a serious medical event. Most dogs develop the condition over time with obese dogs and older dogs most seriously affected. The condition is medically managed in most dogs. Surgery can repair a badly collapsed trachea, but it is a tricky surgery saved for the worst cases. This condition is generally thought to be genetic in Yorkies. There is no genetic test for it yet. Owners of the breed should not use collars or stress the neck (windpipe) of the dog.

Dr. Karen Tobias at the University of Tennessee has written extensively about liver conditions prevalent in the Yorkshire terrier. The risk of liver shunts in Yorkshire terrier has been reported to be as high as thirty-six times that of all breeds combined. The liver filters the blood of toxins. In a portosystemic shunt, a dog lacks the blood vessels leading to the liver resulting in toxins remaining in the animal's blood. Dogs with this condition can become very ill. They often lose weight. They may, also, have seizures. This congenital problem stunts the development of puppies and its symptoms usually become more pronounced as the dog ages. The condition is treated medically and with a special diet. Severe cases require surgery. The evidence is highly suggestive of a genetic root to the condition, but there is currently no genetic test for it.

SENSITIVE DIGESTIVE SYSTEMS

Yorkies are known for having sensitive digestive systems. Yorkie breeders should feed a high-quality kibble. Dogs that exhibit digestive problems especially ones that get worse or do not seem to get better with better quality food should be thoroughly evaluated by a veterinarian. Liver shunts (as discussed above) do cause problems with the digestion. The problem is so common that the marketplace provides dog food for those dogs suffering from liver issues.

HYPOGLYCEMIA

Hypoglycemia means low blood sugar. It is caused by the pancreas not producing enough insulin for the body's metabolism. Dogs with the condition may be lethargic, tremble, not eat, show a lack of coordination, and, if left untreated, may lose consciousness. Untreated hypoglycemia can result in death. Yorkie puppies under three months are particularly susceptible to the condition, but all toy dogs run a risk. Hypoglycemia can be treated by meal management and awareness of the owner. Several small meals may be advised for toys that show radical spikes and valleys in their blood glucose levels.

LEGG-CALVE-PERTHES

Legg-Calve-Perthes disease is cropping up in the Yorkshire Terrier breed. In Legg-Calve-Perthes, the blood supply to the femur bone of the leg gets cut off. The bone tissue then dies. The irregularity in the structure of the femur causes leg problems like pain and lameness. It is a condition that first strikes puppies at about 6 months of age. Toys and especially Yorkies have high rates of the condition. Treatment involves surgical removal of the dead bone tissue. Research is ongoing in isolating the genes responsible for the condition.

PATELLAR LUXATION

Yorkshire Terriers have a very high incidence of patellar luxation. In this condition, the kneecap of the dog comes out of place. Symptoms include pain, and lameness, becoming “knock-kneed” or suddenly becoming unable to stand. Surgery is the best way to put the kneecap in place and secure it, but the outcomes vary. The initial surgery has a success rate of 90 percent, but approximately half the time the problem recurs. Older dogs which also suffer osteoarthritis in the joint may not have as favorable surgical outcomes.

This is an inherited condition. The Orthopedic Foundation for Animals maintains an extensive database on dogs with the condition. According to OFA information, Yorkshire terriers ranked second only to Pomeranians in incidence rates of patellar luxation. Twenty-three percent of the 828 dogs evaluated were positive for the condition.

HOW TO BREED YORKSHIRE TERRIERS

When breeding Yorkshire terriers, as explained below, there are a lot of risks and inevitable expenses that the breeder must prepare for. All the risks linked to breeding Yorkshire terriers make the price of each puppy go up.

The emotional charge is also huge on the Yorkie breeders which is something to consider if this is going to be your first Yorkshire terrier breeding. Vet bills will also accumulate with most of the interventions generally not covered by dog insurance policies.

AVERAGE SIZE OF THE LITTER

Yorkshire terriers have small litters commensurate with their small size, the puppy count ranges from two to five puppies. The average is four puppies. A larger dam would tend to the higher numbers and smaller ones to the lower ones.

The number of whelps does include all puppies whelped including stillborn and ones that died shortly after birth. The neonatal mortality rate in litters of very small Yorkies (under four pounds) is high. Also, Yorkshire terrier puppies that die after birth oftentimes do so from hypoglycemia (low blood sugar). Breeders of Yorkies need to make sure the puppies are nursing. If a puppy is not adequately nursing, it is very likely that the puppy will become hypoglycemic. Breeders must be ready to step in and bottle feed using high-quality puppy formula.

CESAREAN SECTIONS

Birth complications are high for the breed. The small size of Yorkies necessitates c-sections on a routine basis. It is very important that the size of sires and dams be of the same size. Ideally, a sire would have a history like the breed's progenitor Huddersfield Ben and produce smaller puppies. Of course, mating a small sire with a larger dam could be problematic too.

Extremely small Yorkies simply can't deliver puppies naturally. Small Yorkies, unfortunately, do not tolerate anesthesia well. Death from anesthesia adds to the risk of a cesarean section. Some veterinarians will test a dog's sensitivity prior to a surgical event. This kind of testing should be done prior to pregnancy.

The most common reason for cesarean sections among Toy breeds is size dystocia or the birth canal not being large enough to deliver the puppy. The puppy just gets stuck. Dams which have prolonged labor with no puppy being whelped need immediate veterinary attention.

ALLOWED COLORS AND COLOR PATTERNS

The coat of the Yorkie is one of the main things that make the breed so unique. There are only four acceptable colors. Both the Kennel Club and the AKC standards for the breed require a mature dog have the dark steel blue from the back of the neck to the base of the tail. The tan on the dog is a dark one. Tan hair strands are darkest at their roots and become progressively lighter to the tips.

Yorkie puppies are born dark black or tan. They begin to get their mature coat at about six months. At full maturity, they should have the customarily colored coat. No interspersed colors are permitted on a mature Yorkie. Usually, by a year or two, the coat has reached its mature color. The puppy coat makes a selection of a puppy a bit of an unknown for those hoping to show a dog. Fortunately, Yorkies rarely have unusual coloring or patterns. Those that do are not bred.

EXTREME YORKIE BREEDING

People get excited about small dogs—the smaller the better. The idea of a dog so small it can fit into a pocket goes back to the Victorian age. The breed standard sets a maximum weight of seven pounds as desirable but is silent on a minimum. The implication from the standard, too, is smaller is better. In 2010, a Yorkshire terrier named Lucy got included in the Guinness Book of World Records as the smallest working dog. Lucy, at the time 3 years old, only weighed two and a half pounds and was six inches long. Lucy fits the description of a miniature or teacup Yorkie.

MINIATURE & TEACUP YORKIES

However, the use of the labels teacup and miniature are marketing terms and not recognized by the breed's parent club in the U.S, the AKC, and the KC. The America Yorkshire Terrier Club deems the use of such terms as "teacup" in advertising an ethical violation for its members.

The Kennel Club has taken a very clear stance about not only the health risks to dogs bred so small but also the "unscrupulous" nature of the advertising for them. Extremely small dogs have more fragile bones and have more respiratory problems. The Kennel Club does not set a limit on what ethically is too small, but stresses that breeders should refrain from exaggerating any of the characteristics of the breed standard, including the Yorkshire terrier's size. Smaller is better as long as health is not sacrificed for it. None of the registries accepts teacup

Yorkie or miniature Yorkie as its own breed. These tiny dogs, though, have been around for a long time. Many of the very first conformation shows of the breed in 1878 included classes of Yorkshire terriers under five pounds. A three-to-seven-pound weight, finally, became the norm.

The AKC has been less clear on the subject of extremely small breeding. The AKC has stated it does not "endorse" teacup breeds but does not issue a strong statement like the Kennel Club. The AKC, in general, has been less receptive to restraints on ethical breeders. A smaller but healthy Yorkshire terrier seems to be a possibility for the AKC.

Most commentators recommend a minimum weight of four pounds for a healthy adult Yorkshire terrier. A dog of this weight can have strong bones, breed, and whelp like any of its bigger cousins. Tiny dogs have fragile bones, more hip dysplasia, and other structural diseases, and are more at risk for cesarean sections and death from anesthesia. Litter sizes of dogs under four pounds average of two puppies. These small puppies have a high risk of not surviving to reach the weaning stage. Tiny Yorkie puppies are at extremely high risk of death from hypoglycemia.

YORKIE HYBRIDS AND CROSSBREEDS

The Yorkshire terrier has been the basis of other types of dogs that became breeds in their own right. For example, at the turn of the 20th century, the Yorkshire terrier was outcrossed and bred with the Australian Silky terrier. Australian breeders touted a new breed of dog, but it took five decades before the Australian Silky terrier was finally recognized by the AKC as its own breed in 1959.

Another example is the Biewer Terrier which has only been recognized as its own breed since 2014. Thirty years before, the Biewer terrier started out as a Yorkshire terrier with coat colors of blue, white, and gold. This nonconforming Yorkshire Terrier had such a great look to its owner (Mrs. Biewer) that she spent her lifetime breeding these dogs. Other people loved the look and —as it happens in the dog breeding world— a new breed was created.

Fourteen crosses of the Yorkshire terrier have been bred for one reason or another. Sometimes a breeder will be responding to a public demand like making a great looking dog have flopping ears rather than upright ones, or for a coat to become less of an allergy problem. For example, a cross of a Yorkshire terrier with a Chihuahua makes a

Chorkie. The improvements made over either breed may be in a small size but with an exceptionally soft and silky coat.

Other common crosses include the Morkie (Maltese cross) and Yorkipoo (Poodle cross). None of these crosses are recognized by any of the breed clubs. These crosses are frequently advertised and sold online. Many of these small crosses that are sold en masse online originate in puppy mills. Most designer dogs lack the thoughtful breeding that will turn it into a recognized breed. Puppy mills rarely, if ever, make their breeding stock undergo health checks so buyers are putting themselves in a delicate situation of having to shell out thousands of dollars in a few years' time.

FUTURE OF YORKIE BREEDING

The breeding of Yorkshire terrier dogs is divisive. Mainly because original fanciers of the breed are defending the original look of the breed, while newer owners and breeders are keener on a smaller and trendier type of Yorkshire terriers. The future of Yorkie breeding should normally go in two different directions over the next years.

The breed will remain as it is today with its normal healthy size. Yorkshire terriers have always been loved and will always be loved for their peculiar coat and look. The slow decrease in popularity may boost the other breeders, preferring a smaller size and a more viral look even if this means giving up on the official registration as purebred Yorkshire.

A lot of hybrid breedings are happening and Yorkshire terriers are also part of these crosses; we can expect a lot more of them over the next years. The general public is now less enamored with purebred dogs. Hybrid and designer dogs are often preferred over purebred dogs, allowing breeders to trial new crosses as often as they think is necessary.

PROS AND CONS OF YORKSHIRE TERRIERS

The Good

- Fine-boned, elegant, easy to carry, doesn't take up much space
- Sheds very lightly (one of the best breeds for allergy sufferers)

- Lively and inquisitive, moves swiftly with light-footed grace
- Doesn't need a lot of exercise
- A keen watchdog – won't fail to announce strangers
- Peaceful with other pets

The Bad

- Physically fragile, requiring a great deal of supervision and monitoring
- Notorious housebreaking difficulties
- Prone to barking
- Regular brushing and combing, or regularly trimming/clipping the coat short
- Suspiciousness, shrillness, and nastiness when babied or spoiled or not socialized enough or made to behave

WHAT IS THE BEST AGE TO BUY A YORKIE PUPPY?

If you are seeking a family pet a reputable Yorkshire Terrier Breeder will not release a puppy to a new home before it is twelve (12) weeks old. This ensures the puppy is old enough to have had some of its shots, has been checked by a veterinarian, and a health certificate issued. The puppy's ears should be erect, and you can generally tell what size the puppy will be at maturity when it is twelve weeks old by doubling the weight. Although not a definite rule it is generally thought that if a twelve week old Yorkie puppy is three pounds it will likely be six pounds at maturity. Also, by twelve weeks the puppy should be outgoing and well socialized so it will easily accept the transition of leaving its mother and siblings.

On the other hand, if you are interested in a show potential puppy the time frame should be much different. You need to start your search well in advance of actually selecting a puppy. Nothing beats doing research, going to local dog shows, reading as much as you can about the breed, and talking to as many show breeders as possible. There is no way to guarantee a definite yorkie show dog before it is nine or ten months old, and its actually uncertain until you get that first winning ribbon many months later. Yorkies go through a tremendous transition from puppy to adulthood in coat condition, stature, personality, and demeanor. But one of the most important goals is gaining the confidence of the breeder because no show breeder is going to release a good show puppy to a novice who cannot fulfill the puppy's potential. By the time a show potential puppy is nine or ten months old, the personality will be outgoing, the terrier spirit portrayed, and it will be leash trained. The coat will have the correct silky texture, and the color will be coming in clearly. You will be able to tell by the gait if the puppy has good structure, and by then the puppy teeth will be replacing with permanent mature denture so you can tell if the bite is correct. In other words, you can see the real potential in front of you. From then on, its up to you to continue ring training and not let the breeder down.

CONCLUSION

The Yorkshire Terrier's heritage can be seen in their sharp, intelligent expression, confident carriage, and compact body. They a small breed, however, now more noted for their long, silky hair, which is often fine, glossy, and perfectly straight. Their color is a hallmark of this breed, with the blue a dark steel blue and the tan a clear tan.

www.ingramcontent.com/pod-product-compliance
Ingram Content Group UK Ltd.
Pitfield, Milton Keynes, MK11 3LW, UK
UKHW021655190726
13853UKWH00001B/276

9 798423 943417